BARI TASTY BITES!

40 easy bite-size recipes to keep the weight off after bariatric surgery

Your Onederland

Bariatric Community, Education & Support

THESE BITES ARE FOR YOU

You didn't take the easy way out, choosing bariatric surgery to steer your life in a new direction. Because changing your habits for the long run is *hard work* to say the least.

Making the right food choices is an important part of your bariatric journey and *Bari Tasty Bites!* can be your companion when choosing a bariatric friendly snack that will fit your needs.

Enjoying food after Bariatric Surgery is 100% possible and it's what we want for you too!

With 40 bariatric friendly bite-size recipes you'll find something to nibble on and find the inspiration that you deserve.

DISCLAIMER

This book is made for educational, entertaining and inspirational purposes only and is not intended as personal or medical advice.

By reading this document, the reader acknowledges that the information provided in this book is not intended as nutritional, clinical, medical, legal or financial advice. Always consult a licensed specialist before attempting any techniques presented in this book.

All effort has been made to provide correct, accurate and up to date information. No warranties of any kind are declared or implied.

By reading this document, the reader agrees that under no circumstances the author is responsible for any direct or indirect losses, as a result of the use of information of this document, including but not limited to inaccuracies, omissions or errors of any kind.

CONTENTS

INTRODUCTION

Up until this day, bariatric surgery is the most effective treatment for morbid obesity worldwide.

But just because it's effective, doesn't mean that it won't be challenging.

Navigating your post-op life isn't easy - and making the right food choices can be a daunting task.

That's why we wanted to create something meaningful to help you find inspiration when it comes to your food choices. And what better way than to start with bariatric friendly snack recipes, that will help you meet your goals?

This book starts with a few important pointers about eating after bariatric surgery - discussing the key macronutrient protein and slider foods for example. Next, you'll find 5 chapters dedicated to a specific snack category; Savory, Sweet, Crunchy, Frozen and Portable.

Before you try anything new, make sure that you're cleared by your surgeon to do so.

Most recipes in Bari Tasty Bites! are suitable for 6+ months post-op.

With that being said, enjoy the recipes you'll find in here and all the best on your bariatric journey!

A FRESH START

Bariatric Surgery isn't about losing weight fast - it's about creating habits that last. From your very first pre-op appointment to your maintenance stage - your bariatric journey will be a dynamic one.

There will be ups and downs - highs and lows. But in between dealing with the physical changes and creating a new bariatric mindset - a whole new life awaits.

A life where you can be your best self without anything or anyone holding you back. Here's to a fresh start!

How to use this book

First, we'll dive into some basic principles to help you understand your hunger and fullness cues better, like:

- Protein
- Bariatric Snacks vs Slider Foods
- Recognizing your Bariatric Fullness Cues

Next- you'll find 40 delicious bariatric friendly bites to help you feel inspired in your bariatric journey. Especially when you feel like having a 'snack' but aren't sure what to eat next.

Most of the bari bites in this book are suitable if you're further out, cleared to eat solids and can tolerate most foods well (approximately from 6 months post-op and onwards)

All recipes include an indication of the nutrition facts and a suggested serving size which you can adjust to your own personal preference.

Always follow the portion size that fits your needs.

And don't worry - we'll explain how to recognize your bariatric fullness cues in the next chapter too!

Some motivation before we start

We want to reiterate that bariatric surgery is NOT the easy way out. And it's not cheating either. Making the right food choices is only part of your post-op lifestyle.

It's *changing your habits* that's going to be the most difficult, but also the most rewarding part of your journey.

Change is hard. Change is beautiful. Change is inevitable.

Just remember that you can do hard things and you didn't come this far to only come this far!

3 BARIATRIC BASICS

One of the key nutrients after bariatric surgery is protein. But other nutrients like fiber, coming mostly from complex carb food sources, are invaluable too. And we can't forget about those healthy fats neither.

In this book, we don't demonize foods. Instead, we focus on *balance*. Nutrition after bariatric surgery has to be sustainable and realistic.

By the end of this chapter you know the basics about protein, slider foods and how to recognize your fullness cues.

Protein

Protein. It's one of the key macronutrients after bariatric surgery. Will it be easy meeting your protein goals? No, it most definitely won't. But is it necessary to try the best you possibly can to get that protein in? Yes, it is!

Why you need protein after Bariatric Surgery

Protein is involved in all sorts of vital processes in your body and is an essential nutrient to support your overall health. Protein is a substantial part of body tissue varying from skin, organs and your muscles. Additionally, protein plays a significant role in hormone and enzyme functions.

Protein consists of different types of blocks called amino acids. In total, there are 20 different types of amino acids, 9 of which your body can't make on its own. Therefore, you need high-protein food sources to make sure you're getting all the amino acids in.

In order to recover swiftly after Bariatric Surgery, your body needs protein to heal. And it's normal that you won't meet your daily protein goals all at once.

After bariatric surgery, you slowly start to introduce new textures to your diet. There are different types of food sources (and protein supplements) that can help you meet your goals.

High Protein Food Sources

Not all protein is created equal. Protein comes in different shapes and forms.

Let's look at some examples:

- Protein from solid foods
- Protein from liquids
- Protein from animal products
- Protein from plant-based products
- Protein from supplements such as protein powder and protein bars

Protein is helpful for:

- Post-op recovery
- Curbing appetite
- Maintaining muscle mass
- Suppressing ghrelin (your hunger hormone)

Protein from most animal-based products is considered complete protein, as they contain (enough) of all 9 essential amino acids your body can't make on its own. (Semi-)complete protein from plant-based products are soy, quinoa, hemp and chia seeds.

On the next page we've laid out a few of the most common high-protein food sources.

Table 1. High Protein Food Sources categorized by origin

Animal Based

- Chicken
- Turkey
- Beef
- Pork
- Lamb (high in fat)
- Veal
- Tuna
- Tilapia
- Flounder
- Salmon
- Mackerel
- Sea bass
- Red snapper
- Lobster
- Egg
- All cheeses
- Cottage cheese

- Yogurt
- Quark
- Greek yogurt
- Milk
- Buttermilk

Plant Based

- Tofu
- Tempeh
- Edamame
- Nuts
- Hemp seeds
- Chia seeds
- Flax seeds
- Soy milk
- Soy yogurt
- Vegan cheese
- Seitan

- Lentils
- Peas
- Beans
- Amaranth
- Quinoa
- Pumpkin seeds
- Hemp hearts

Supplement Based

- Whey powder
- Casein powder
- All protein powders
- Protein bars
- Protein shakes

Bariatric Snacks vs Slider Foods

Although slider foods aren't an official workbook term in the field of nutrition, it's safe to say that we can refer to slider foods as high-carbohydrate foods, predominantly refined sugars, that offer little to no nutritional value. They're low in fiber and/or protein and won't keep your small stomach full for long.

Slider foods are often also the more 'snacky' foods like chips, pretzels and popcorn. These types of foods can be a pitfall after bariatric surgery as they take little time to digest and easily *slide* through your small stomach to the rest of your digestive system.

We're not going to demonize foods or call them 'bad foods' - but it's important to be aware of their physiological effects.

After bariatric surgery, your food passes from your small stomach to your digestive system quicker. And slider foods facilitate this process, because they're easier to digest.

Now, we're not saying that you can't eat slider foods anymore. But it's all about *balance* - just like we're going to show you in this book.

Pairing a slider food with a high fiber or high protein source not only helps you ditch the 'all-or-nothing mindset' - it'll make your small meal more delicious as well.

Bariatric Fullness Cues

Small stomach, fewer concerns? We don't think so! It can be pretty challenging to understand your appetite and fullness cues better once you had Bariatric Surgery.

But why is that?

Bariatric surgery not only restricts the amount of food you can eat in one sitting by reducing your stomach's capacity. It also changes the way your hunger hormones are regulated.

Bariatric Surgery is a *metabolic surgery* and impacts your metabolism big time.

One of your hunger hormones is called *ghrelin* and is mainly produced in the upper part of your stomach. All bariatric surgery types (except laparoscopic gastric banding) will either remove or bypass a great part of the production sites of ghrelin.

This often results in less appetite and quicker satiety.

But it's not always as simple as 'just feeling full'. You may find it hard to gauge your portion size and to know when to start or stop eating.

Below, you'll find examples of the most common (physical) appetite and fullness cues to look out for.

Examples of Appetite & Fullness Cues

Here are a few examples that can help you understand your own cues better:

Signs of Appetite	Signs of Fullness
Hunger Pangs	Burping
Weakness	Coughing
Fatigue	"Feeling Full"
Light Headedness	Sneezing
Little Energy	Runny Nose
	Hiccups
	Sighing

Getting familiar with your new stomach takes time - and it's okay if things don't go as planned straight off the bat.

You will forget to eat. You will overeat. You will eat something that sits well one day - while it can make you feel sick another. Things can be confusing.

It's all part of the post-op progress. Even years later you may find some things happening that you can't really put your finger on.

Always be sure to follow your surgeon's guidelines and ask for support if you have unanswered questions.

Now, to sum everything up - we've covered 3 bariatric basics (protein, slider foods and fullness cues) that are relevant to the main reason you've put your hands on this book - having great snacks at hand to keep you full and satisfied.

So, let's start with our favorite bite sized bariatric recipes!

SAVORY
BITES

Ricotta Zucchini Fritters

⚔ Yield: 4 servings

🕐 Time: 45 minutes

☑ Solid Foods

☑ Soft Foods

☐ Pureed Foods

☐ Full Liquids

Ingredients

- 1 medium zucchini, shredded
- 1 teaspoon salt
- 1/4 cup (25 g) fresh scallion, chopped
- 1/2 teaspoon garlic powder
- 1/2 teaspoon ground black pepper
- 1/2 cup (75 g) ricotta
- 1/4 cup (25 g) grated Parmesan cheese
- 1 egg
- 1/4 cup (35 g) all-purpose flour
- 2 tablespoons vegetable oil

Toppings (optional)
- Chopped dill
- Greek yogurt (dip)
- Lemon wedges

Nutrition Facts
Per Serving

153 calories
Protein 7.2 g
Carbs 8.1 g
Fiber 0.8 g
Fat 10 g

Directions

1. In a colander, add zucchini and salt. Let the zucchini drain, about 20 minutes.
2. Squeeze all the excess moisture from the zucchini and place in a mixing bowl.
3. Add scallion, garlic powder, black pepper, ricotta and Parmesan. Taste and add more seasoning or salt if needed.
4. Add the egg and flour. Stir until well combined.
5. Place a cooling rack over a baking sheet.
6. Heat oil over medium heat.
7. Add a 2-tablespoon mound into the pan. Gently flatten the zucchini mounds. Bake on both sides until golden brown.
8. Repeat this process until all batter is used.
9. Let the fritters cool off on the cooling rack before serving.
10. Serve with Greek yogurt dip, lemon wedges and chopped dill.

Recipe Notes

- Peel the zucchini before shredding if you're still in the soft food stage. And make sure the texture is smooth. Omit the scallion.
- Substitute shredded zucchini for shredded carrots.
- You can also use an air fryer or oven instead of a pan to bake the zucchini fritters. Bake on 350°F (180°C).

Beef Taco Bites

✗ Yield: 12 servings

🕐 Time: 35 minutes

☑ Solid Foods   ☐ Pureed Foods

☐ Soft Foods   ☐ Full Liquids

Ingredients

- 1 lb. (455 g) lean ground beef
- 3 tablespoons taco seasoning
- 6 oz (170 g) diced tomato
- 1 1/2 (150 g) cups shredded cheddar cheese
- 6 large whole wheat tortillas
- 1 tablespoon olive oil

Directions

1. In a skillet, cook the ground beef, about 8 minutes.
2. Add taco seasoning and tomatoes. Stir until well combined.
3. Preheat oven to 375°F (190°C)
4. Cut flour tortillas into squares and cut each into 4 smaller equally sized squares.
5. Coat a muffin tin with non-stick cooking spray.
6. Line each cup of a prepared muffin tin with a tortilla sheet.
7. Add 1 1/2 tablespoons beef mixture. Press down and place another layer of tortilla sheet, then a second layer of beef mixture and top off with the cheese.
8. Lightly brush the top edges of the tortilla with olive oil.
9. Place in oven and bake until edges are light brown, about 20 minutes.

Nutrition Facts
Per Serving

197 calories
Protein 12.8 g
Carbs 11.2 g
Fiber 0.9 g
Fat 11 g

Recipe Notes

- Serve with sour cream and cilantro.
- Substitute ground beef for ground turkey if you can't tolerate beef well.
- If you don't have taco seasoning try this combination of herbs instead: garlic powder, onion powder, salt, ground paprika, crushed red pepper flakes and oregano.

Avocado Deviled Eggs

Yield: 3 servings

Time: 15 minutes

 Solid Foods

✓ Soft Foods

✓ Pureed Foods (see recipe notes)

☐ Full Liquids

Ingredients

- 3 eggs
- 1 avocado, peeled and pitted
- 1 tablespoon lime juice
- 1/4 cup (25 g) fresh scallion, chopped
- Salt and pepper to taste

Directions

1. Boil the eggs, about 10 minutes.
2. Peel the eggs and carefully cut them lengthways in half. Remove the yolk from the eggs.
3. In a bowl, add egg yolks and avocado. Mash until softened.
4. Stir in the chopped onion, lime juice, salt and pepper.
5. Scoop the yolk and avocado mixture into the egg white halves.
6. Serve immediately.

Nutrition Facts
Per Serving

176 calories
Protein 7.3 g
Carbs 1.1 g
Fiber 1.9 g
Fat 15.4 g

Recipe Notes

- The filling of this snack, without the scallion and lime, is also suitable for the pureed stage - *if tolerated well and approved by your surgeon.*
- Omit the scallion if you're still on soft foods.
- Use a piping bag if you want to present the deviled eggs more neatly.

Basic Bariatric Chaffles

🍴 Yield: 2 servings

🕐 Time: 10 minutes

☑ Solid Foods   ☐ Pureed Foods

☐ Soft Foods   ☐ Full Liquids

Ingredients

- 2 eggs
- 1 cup (100 g) mozzarella, finely shredded

Toppings (optional)
- Fresh fruit
- Zero-sugar syrup
- Marinara & boiled egg
- Roasted vegetables

Directions

1. Preheat waffle maker.
2. In a bowl, crack the eggs and whisk with a fork. Add the mozzarella and stir until combined.
3. Spray the waffle iron with non-stick cooking spray.
4. Pour half of the mixture into the heated waffle iron and bake, about 3 minutes.
5. Remove waffle and repeat with remaining batter.
6. Serve warm.

Nutrition Facts
Per Serving

191 calories
Protein 15.5 g
Carbs 0.4 g
Fiber 0 g
Fat 14.2 g

Recipe Notes

- Add toppings like fresh fruit or something savory like roasted veggies to your chaffles.
- Substitute mozzarella for a different cheese such as ricotta or grated cheddar.
- Let your chaffles cool off and pack as lunch for work.

Black Bean Dip

 Yield: 8 servings

Time: 10 minutes

☑ Solid Foods
☑ Soft Foods

☑ Pureed Foods (just the beans, refried)
☐ Full Liquids

Ingredients

- 2 1/2 cups (425 g) black beans, canned
- 1/2 cup (130 g) tomato salsa
- 1 garlic clove, minced
- 2 teaspoons lemon juice
- 1/4 teaspoons cumin powder
- 2 teaspoons cilantro, chopped
- Salt and pepper to taste

Directions

1. Drain and rinse the black beans.
2. In a food processor, add the beans, salsa, garlic, lemon juice, cumin and half of the cilantro . Blend until smooth.
3. Transfer black bean mixture into serving bowl. Top with rest of cilantro and add salt and pepper to taste.
4. Serve with pita bread, tortilla chips or raw veggies.

Nutrition Facts
Per Serving

45 calories
Protein 2.7 g
Carbs 6.3 g
Fiber 2.9 g
Fat 0.4 g

Recipe Notes

- Did you know that legumes are relatively higher in complex carbs? But also offer protein and other valuable nutrients like iron.
- This dip also works great as a spread on toast or crackers.
- Grab a small container and bring your dip to go, along with your favorite raw veggie sticks (eg. celery sticks, carrot sticks). Add an extra splash of lemon juice for prolonged freshness.

Stuffed Egg Portobello

Yield: 4 servings

Time: 30 minutes

☑ Solid Foods
☐ Soft Foods

☐ Pureed Foods
☐ Full Liquids

Ingredients

- 4 large portobello mushroom caps
- 4 eggs
- Salt and pepper to taste

For garnish (optional)
- Basil leaves
- Grated Parmesan
- Nutritional yeast (vegan alternative for cheese)

Directions

1. Preheat the oven to 400°F (200°C).
2. Line a baking sheet with parchment paper.
3. Place the portobello caps on a baking sheet, gill side up.
4. Sprinkle the portobello caps with salt and pepper and bake, about 10 minutes.
5. Remove the portobello caps from the oven.
6. Crack each egg into the portobello cap and sprinkle with salt and pepper.
7. Place portobellos with eggs back in oven and bake, about 15 minutes.
8. Garnish with basil leaves and grated Parmesan.

Nutrition Facts
Per Serving

80 calories
Protein 7.7 g
Carbs 1 g
Fiber 2.1 g
Fat 4.6 g

Recipe Notes

- Did you know that portobellos are rich in fiber, selenium and vitamin B2?
- Add grated cheddar on top of the cracked egg before putting the portobello in the oven for a crispy crust.
- Add 1 tablespoon of grated cheese on top of the egg before placing the portobello in the oven if you enjoy cheese.

Baked Cheese Sticks

✕ Yield: 6 servings

🕐 Time: 20 minutes
Freezing time: 1 hour

☑ Solid Foods   ☐ Pureed Foods
☐ Soft Foods   ☐ Full Liquids

Ingredients

- 6 string cheese sticks
- 1 egg
- 1/4 cup (35 g) almond flour
- 1/4 cup (25 g) powdered Parmesan cheese
- 1/4 teaspoon oregano
- 1/4 teaspoon onion powder
- 1/4 teaspoon garlic powder
- 1/4 teaspoon ground black pepper
- 1/4 teaspoon salt

Directions

1. Cut string cheese sticks in half, crosswise.
2. In a bowl, beat the egg. Set aside.
3. In a freezer-safe ziplock bag, place almond flour, Parmesan, oregano, onion powder, garlic powder, black pepper and salt. Shake well.
4. Dip the cheese sticks in the egg mixture.
5. Next, place the cheese sticks in the ziplock bag and coat them by gently shaking the bag.
6. Leave the cheese sticks in the bag and freeze for at least 1 hour.
7. Preheat oven to 400°F (200°C).
8. Line a baking sheet with parchment paper.
9. Remove the cheese sticks from freezer and place them on the baking sheet.
10. Bake in oven, about 7 minutes or until golden brown.

Nutrition Facts
Per Serving

57 calories
Protein 6 g
Carbs 2.1 g
Fiber 0.6 g
Fat 2.7 g

Recipe Note

- You can use an air fryer instead of an oven too. Use the same temperature and cooking time.
- Serve the cheese sticks with a warm marinara dipping sauce.
- Or try a Greek yogurt dip if you want to add more protein to your snack.

Egg White Bites

Yield: 9 servings

Time: 30 minutes

☑ Solid Foods   ☐ Pureed Foods

☑ Soft Foods   ☐ Full Liquids

Ingredients

- 1 cup (240 ml) egg whites
- 4 eggs, whole
- 1/2 cup (110 g) cottage cheese
- 1/4 cup (25 g) fresh scallion, chopped
- 1/4 teaspoon salt
- 1/2 teaspoon ground black pepper

Topping (optional)
- Chopped scallion

Directions

1. Preheat oven to 350°F (175°C).
2. Spray a 9-cup muffin mold with non-stick cooking spray.
3. In a blender, add the egg whites, eggs and cottage cheese. Blend until smooth.
4. In a bowl, add egg mixture and scallion, salt and pepper. Stir until well combined.
5. Pour mixture into muffin molds. Fill each cup about 3/4.
6. Bake in preheated oven until egg white bites are set, about 18 minutes.
7. Garnish with chopped scallion.

Nutrition Facts
Per Serving

39 calories
Protein 5.1 g
Carbs 0.3 g
Fiber 0 g
Fat 1.9 g

Recipe Note

- Optionally add finely chopped bell pepper and spinach to the egg mixture before pouring it into the muffin molds.
- Substitute cottage cheese for shredded mozzarella if you don't like cottage cheese. But keep in mind that cottage cheese has more protein and less fat than mozzarella.
- Omit the scallion if you're still in the soft foods stage.

Tuna Avocado Boats

Yield: 2 servings

Time: 10 minutes

☑ Solid Foods
☑ Soft Foods

☑ Pureed Foods (see recipe notes)
☐ Full Liquids

Ingredients

- 5 oz (140 g) canned tuna, in brine
- 1 avocado, peeled
- 1 teaspoon lemon juice
- 1/4 small red onion, finely chopped
- Salt and pepper to taste

Directions

1. Drain the tuna.
2. Slice avocado in half and remove the pit.
3. With a spoon, carefully scoop out the avocado, leaving the peel in whole.
4. Chop the avocado into small cubes.
5. In a bowl, add avocado cubes, tuna, squeezed lemon, red onion, salt and pepper. Mix until well combined.
6. Take avocado peel halves and scoop half of tuna mixture in one avocado half. Scoop the remaining tuna mixture in other avocado half.

Nutrition Facts
Per Serving

248 calories
Protein 19.4 g
Carbs 2.3 g
Fiber 3.1 g
Fat 17.3 g

Recipe Notes

- Omit the onion and lemon juice when still in the pureed/soft foods stage. Blend the filling well.
- Did you know that avocado is a great source of unsaturated fats that can help you curb appetite?
- Try the filling of this recipe on whole wheat toast or as a dip with pita bread.
- If the avocado peel easily breaks, put the tuna mixture in serving bowls instead of the peels.

Crispy Air Fryer Wings

🍴 Yield: 8 servings

🕐 Time: 40 minutes

☑ Solid Foods

☐ Soft Foods

☐ Pureed Foods

☐ Full Liquids

Ingredients

- 1 1/2 lbs (680 g) chicken wings
- 3 teaspoons Cajun seasoning

Dipping sauces (optional)
- Greek yogurt
- Marinara sauce

Directions

1. Pat the chicken wings dry with a paper towel.
2. In a bowl, mix the chicken wings with the Cajun seasoning until fully coated.
3. Place the seasoned chicken wings in a preheated air fryer on 350°F (175°C), about 35 minutes or until crisp and browned.
4. Serve immediately.

Nutrition Facts
Per Serving

159 calories
Protein 24.2 g
Carbs 0.5 g
Fiber 0 g
Fat 6.7 g

Recipe Notes

- If you don't have an air fryer, use the oven instead. Bake at same temperature, same cooking time.
- Paprika powder, onion powder, garlic powder and ground black pepper make an excellent combination of flavors.
- Serve with a low-fat Greek yogurt dip and celery sticks.

Crispy Tofu Nuggets

Yield: 5 servings

Time: 50 minutes

☑ Solid Foods ☐ Pureed Foods

☐ Soft Foods ☐ Full Liquids

POST-OP

NORMALIZING CARBS

Ingredients

- 14 oz (400 g) extra firm tofu
- 1 cup (110 g) breadcrumbs
- 2 tablespoons vegetable oil
- 1 teaspoon paprika powder
- 1 teaspoon salt
- 1/4 teaspoon ground black pepper
- 1/2 teaspoon garlic powder
- 1/4 teaspoon dried parsley
- 2 tablespoons corn starch
- 1 1/2 cup (350 ml) soy milk
- 1 teaspoon lemon juice

Nutrition Facts
Per Serving

252 calories
Protein 8 g
Carbs 32 g
Fiber 4 g
Fat 8 g

Directions

1. Preheat oven to 355°F (180°C).
2. Wrap the tofu in a paper towel and carefully squeeze out the extra water. Slice the tofu into five 1/2 inch parts. Gently break each part into 4 nuggets using your hands. Set aside.
3. In a bowl add soy milk and lemon juice. Whisk well.
4. In a second bowl, add corn starch. Set aside.
5. In a skillet, toast the breadcrumbs while stirring until golden brown. Remove from skillet and place in another bowl.
6. Add the paprika powder, salt, pepper, garlic powder and parsley to the breadcrumbs and stir until well combined.
7. To coat the tofu, place a nugget in the corn starch. Make sure the nugget is completely coated.
8. Next, place the coated nugget in the soy milk mixture. Remove and allow the excess liquid to drip back into the bowl. Now place the coated nugget back into the corn starch.
9. Coat the nugget in corn starch again and then next back into the soy milk mixture. Place the coated nugget into the breadcrumbs and toss making sure the nugget is fully coated. Place nugget on baking sheet.
10. Repeat step 7 through 9 with the remaining tofu until they're all fully coated and placed on the baking sheet.
11. Place the baking sheet with nuggets in the preheated oven and bake, about 35 minutes. Turning the nuggets halfway through the baking process.
12. Remove the nuggets from the oven and serve immediately with your favorite dipping sauce.

Mini Pita Pizzas

Yield: 4 servings

Time: 25 minutes

☑ Solid Foods ☐ Pureed Foods

☐ Soft Foods ☐ Full Liquids

POST-OP

NORMALIZING CARBS

Ingredients

- 2 pita breads
- 4 tablespoons marinara
- 16 slices deli chicken
- 1/2 medium red bell pepper, finely chopped
- 4 tablespoons Parmesan cheese, grated
- Salt and pepper to taste

Topping (optional)
- Basil leaves

Directions

1. Preheat oven to 350°F (175°C).
2. Slice pita breads fully open so that you have 4 halves.
3. Add 1 tablespoon of marinara on 1 half of pita bread and spread out evenly.
4. Place 4 slices of the deli chicken on top of the marinara.
5. Add 1/4 of the chopped red bell pepper on top of the chicken.
6. Sprinkle 1/2 tablespoon of parmesan on top of the bell pepper.
7. Add salt and pepper.
8. Repeat the process for the remainders of the pita bread halves.
9. Place the 4 halves on an oven tray and bake, about 8-10 minutes.
10. Sprinkle remainder of the Parmesan cheese on all 4 pita halves. And top with the basil leaves.

Nutrition Facts
Per Serving

147 calories
Protein 11.2 g
Carbs 14 g
Fiber 1 g
Fat 4.7 g

Recipe Notes

- Substitute the deli chicken for deli turkey or canned tuna.
- Mix and match different vegetables on your pita pizza, like eggplant, zucchini and mushrooms.
- You can make your own marinara sauce with fresh tomatoes if desired.

Cranberry Goat Cheese Balls

Yield: 9 servings
Time: 15 minutes

☑ Solid Foods
☐ Soft Foods
☐ Pureed Foods
☐ Full Liquids

Ingredients

- 8 oz (225 g) goat cheese
- 3 cloves garlic, minced
- 2 teaspoons Agava syrup
- 1/4 teaspoon ground black pepper
- 1/2 cup (60 g) walnuts, chopped
- 1/2 cup (80 g) dried cranberries
- 1/2 cup (20 g) basil leaves, chopped

Directions

1. In a bowl, add the goat cheese, garlic, agave syrup and pepper. Mix until well combined.
2. In a second bowl, mix the chopped walnuts, dried cranberries and chopped basil leaves.
3. Roll goat cheese into a small ball, using a small scoop or 2 teaspoons.
4. Press goat cheese into the nut mixture, making sure the goat cheese is fully coated.
5. Roll the goat cheese into a ball again and if needed, roll into nut mixture to coat some more.
6. Serve with pretzel sticks.

Nutrition Facts
Per Serving

68 calories
Protein 3 g
Carbs 4 g
Fiber 0.5 g
Fat 5 g

Recipe Notes

- Drizzle with balsamic vinegar before serving.
- Be aware that goat cheese is quite high in (saturated) fat.
- This recipe should yield about 18 cheese balls - but it can be different according to your preferred size of the goat cheese balls.

SWEET BITES

Air Fryer Apple Chips

🍴 Yield: 2 servings

🕐 Time: 10 minutes

☑ Solid Foods

☐ Soft Foods

☐ Pureed Foods

☐ Full Liquids

POST-OP

NORMALIZING CARBS

Ingredients

- 1 Granny Smith apple, peeled sliced and cored
- 1/4 teaspoon cinnamon powder
- 1 pinch salt

Directions

1. In a bowl mix the apple slices, cinnamon powder and salt, until fully coated.
2. Bake the apples in an air fryer set to 250°F (120°C), about 20 minutes or until slightly browned. Rotate the apples every 5 minutes.
3. Cool before serving.

Nutrition Facts
Per Serving

38 calories
Protein 0.2 g
Carbs 8.1 g
Fiber 1.4 g
Fat 0.1 g

Recipe Notes

- Dip in low-fat Greek yogurt dip to add some protein to this snack.
- Peel the apples if you can't tolerate the skin well.
- If you don't have an air fryer, use an oven instead.

Peanut Butter Cookies

🍴 Yield: 12 cookies

🕐 Time: 20 minutes

☑ Solid Foods ☐ Pureed Foods

☐ Soft Foods ☐ Full Liquids

Ingredients

- 1/2 cup (125 g) peanut butter
- 1 banana
- 1 egg
- 1/2 teaspoon vanilla extract

Directions

1. Preheat oven to 350°F (175°C).
2. In a food processor or blender, add the peanut butter, banana, eggs and vanilla-extract. Blend until smooth.
3. Line a baking sheet with parchment paper.
4. Add 1 tablespoon of peanut butter mixture into a 2 inch cooking ring to create even circles.
5. Place baking tray in middle of oven and bake, about 10 minutes.
6. Allow to cool off before serving.

Nutrition Facts

Per Cookie

99 calories
Protein 3.6 g
Carbs 5.4 g
Fiber 1.2 g
Fat 6.7 g

Recipe Notes

- Add one scoop of vanilla protein powder to increase the protein count of this recipe.
- Substitute vanilla extract with cocoa powder.
- Substitute peanut butter with almond butter.
- If you don't have a cooking ring use an ice cream scoop instead.

Apple Pie Parfait

Yield: 1 serving

Time: 10 minutes

☑ Solid Foods

☐ Soft Foods

☐ Pureed Foods

☐ Full Liquids

POST-OP

NORMALIZING CARBS

Ingredients

- 1 apple, peeled, cored and chopped
- 1/4 teaspoon cinnamon powder
- 1/4 teaspoon vanilla extract
- pinch salt
- 1/2 cup (120 g) low-fat Greek yogurt
- 2 small crackers, crushed

Toppings (optional)
- Chopped walnuts
- Chopped almonds
- Chopped pecans

Directions

1. In a bowl, stir in the chopped apple bits, 1/8 teaspoon of cinnamon, vanilla extract and salt until well combined.
2. Microwave until apple bits are softened, about 2 minutes.
3. In a bowl, stir in yogurt and 1/8 teaspoon of cinnamon until well blended.
4. Spoon half the yogurt mixture in a glass, then add half of the apple mixture and repeat with the other halves of the mixtures. Top with the crushed crackers.

Nutrition Facts
Per Serving

147 calories
Protein 10.6 g
Carbs 22.7g
Fiber 2 g
Fat 0.6 g

Recipe Notes

- For variation, substitute the apple for other fruit.
- Top your apple parfait with different nuts, like almonds, pecans and crushed walnuts.
- Omit the crackers and walnuts if you can't tolerate solid foods yet.

Dutch "Poffertjes"

Yield: 4 servings

Time: 15 minutes
Rising Time: 1 hour

☑ Solid Foods
☐ Soft Foods

☐ Pureed Foods
☐ Full Liquids

POST-OP

NORMALIZING CARBS

Ingredients

- 1 1/2 cups (350 ml) skimmed milk, warm
- 2 1/2 teaspoon instant yeast
- 2 cups (240 g) all-purpose flour
- 1 egg
- 2 tablespoons butter, melted
- 1 teaspoon cinnamon powder

To serve (optional)
- Blueberries
- Raspberries
- Strawberries

Directions

1. In a bowl, add the flour, sugar and yeast. Mix and make a well in the center.
2. Pour in the warmed milk and egg and whisk into a batter. Cover with a clean kitchen towel and leave to rise at room temperature.
3. Grease frying pan with the butter over medium heat. Once warmed, add heaping tablespoons of batter into frying pan, using a small egg ring to make even poffertjes.
4. Once bubbles start to pop up, flip the poffertjes one by one.
5. Repeat steps 3 and 4 until all batter is used up.

Nutrition Facts
Per Serving

303 calories
Protein 11.1 g
Carbs 45.8 g
Fiber 1.9 g
Fat 8.1 g

Recipe Notes

- Make sure that the milk isn't boiling when heated. Hot milk will destroy the yeast which makes it impossible to rise the flour mixture.
- Did you know that poffertjes is a typical street food in the Netherlands? And it's pronounced as "puffer-jes".

Bari Berry Chia Pudding

Yield: 4 servings

Time: 15 minutes
Set Time: 1 hour

☑ Solid Foods   ☐ Pureed Foods
☐ Soft Foods   ☐ Full Liquids

Ingredients

For the vanilla chia pudding:
- 1 1/2 cups (370 ml) skimmed milk
- 1 teaspoon agave syrup
- 3 tablespoons chia seeds
- 2 teaspoons vanilla extract
- pinch salt

For the raspberry chia jam:
- 20 raspberries
- 1 teaspoon agave syrup
- 2 tablespoons chia seeds

Optional (to serve)
- Fresh pomegranate
- Fresh raspberries

Directions

1. In a bowl, whisk together the milk, agave syrup, vanilla extract, chia seeds and salt. Set aside.
2. In a second bowl, smash the raspberries with agave syrup until smooth. Stir in the chia seeds and set aside.
3. Whisk chia pudding again before covering.
4. Transfer both mixtures in 2 separate containers and refrigerate to set for at least 1 hour.
5. Once pudding is set, layer both mixtures on top of each other, starting with the jam.
6. To serve, top with fresh pomegranate and raspberries.

Nutrition Facts
Per Serving

83 calories
Protein 5.3 g
Carbs 7.2 g
Fiber 3.8 g
Fat 2.6 g

Recipe Notes

- Did you know that chia seeds are an excellent source of fiber with nearly 5 grams of fiber per tablespoon?
- Chia seeds contain quercetin, an antioxidant that has cardiovascular benefits.
- Omit the chia seeds if you're still in the pureed stage.

Easy Fruit Skewers

Yield: 12 servings

Time: 15 minutes

☑ Solid Foods   ☐ Pureed Foods

☐ Soft Foods   ☐ Full Liquids

POST-OP

NORMALIZING CARBS

Ingredients

- 1 banana
- 2 kiwis
- 12 strawberries
- 12 grapes
- 2 tangerines

Directions

1. Peel the banana and cut into 12 equal slices.
2. Peel the kiwis and cut into 12 equal quarters.
3. Peel the tangerine and divide the parts.
4. Cut off the the top of the strawberries and cut lengthwise in half.
5. Peel the tangerine and break in parts.
6. Thread the banana slices, kiwi quarters, strawberry halves, grapes and tangerine on skewers.
7. Arrange the skewers on a platter to serve.

Nutrition Facts
Per Serving

34 calories
Protein 0 g
Carbs 6.9 g
Fiber 0.9 g
Fat 0 g

Recipe Notes

- Use all your favorite fruits to make different skewer varieties.
- Want to add some protein to this snack? Add Gouda cheese cubers between each piece of fruit.
- Soften the fruit in microwave first, if desired.

Cottage Cheese Date Boats

Yield: 10 servings

Time: 10 minutes

☑ Solid Foods ☐ Pureed Foods
☐ Soft Foods ☐ Full Liquids

Ingredients

- 10 large Medjool dates, pitted
- 2 tablespoons cottage cheese
- 1 tablespoon almonds, crushed

Directions

1. Place the dates on a plate and gently open them without letting them fall apart.
2. With a teaspoon, fill the dates with cottage cheese.
3. Top with crushed almonds.

Nutrition Facts
Per Serving

33 calories
Protein 0.8 g
Carbs 4.6 g
Fiber 0.6 g
Fat 1.2 g

Recipe Notes

- Did you know that dates are jam packed with fiber - which is much needed after bariatric surgery to support healthy bowel movements.
- Medjool dates originated in the Middle East and North Africa. They're larger in comparison to other dates.

CRUNCHY
BITES

Simple PB & Apple Snack

Yield: 6 servings
Time: 10 minutes

- ☑ Solid Foods
- ☐ Soft Foods
- ☐ Pureed Foods
- ☐ Full Liquids

Ingredients

- 1 large apple
- 3 tablespoons peanut butter

Toppings (optional)
- Oats
- Granola
- Raisins
- Chopped pecans

Directions

1. Slice the apples horizontally so that you are slicing through the core.
2. Match the apple slices that are most similar in size.
3. Remove the core from the centre of the apple slices.
4. Spread 1 tablespoon of peanut butter on one slice of a matching pair.
5. Place the other slice of the matching pair on top of the slice with peanut butter.
6. Repeat until all slices are finished.

Nutrition Facts
Per Serving

62 calories
Protein 1.8 g
Carbs 3.5 g
Fiber 1.1 g
Fat 4.3 g

Recipe Notes

- Add different toppings to the peanut butter to make your snack more nutritious.
- Substitute apple for banana coins and adjust the amount of peanut butter accordingly.
- If you can't tolerate the apple peel - peel the apple before getting started.

Roasted Chickpeas

🍴 Yield: 6 servings

🕐 Time: 30 minutes

☑ Solid Foods ☐ Pureed Foods

☐ Soft Foods ☐ Full Liquids

Ingredients

- 15 oz (425 g) canned chickpeas
- 1 tablespoon olive oil
- 1/2 teaspoon salt

Seasonings (optional)
- 1-2 teaspoons herbs and spices (eg. cumin, paprika, thyme, rosemary, chili powder)

Directions

1. Preheat the oven to 400°F (200°C).
2. Rinse and drain chickpeas.
3. Dry chickpeas thoroughly, yet carefully, using a clean cloth or paper towels.
4. Add olive oil and salt and toss the chickpeas making sure they're evenly coated.
5. Spread chickpeas on a baking sheet and place on a tray in the middle of the oven, about 25 minutes.
6. Add your favorite herbs and spices to the toasted chickpeas and spread evenly.

Nutrition Facts
Per Serving

114 calories
Protein 5.6 g
Carbs 12.7 g
Fiber 5.1 g
Fat 3.4 g

Recipe Notes

- You can also use a skillet instead of the oven to roast the chickpeas. Make sure to toss them regularly to prevent them from burning.
- You could also add the herbs and spices before placing the chickpeas in the oven. Make sure that they don't burn by tossing the chickpeas regularly.

Crunchy Popcorn Chicken

✂ Yield: 8 servings

🕐 Time: 45 minutes

☑ Solid Foods ☐ Pureed Foods

☐ Soft Foods ☐ Full Liquids

Ingredients

- 1 lb. (455 g) chicken breast, cut into small cubes
- 2 eggs
- 1/2 cup (120 ml) buttermilk
- 1/2 cup (60 g) all-purpose flour
- 1/2 cup (60 g) breadcrumbs
- 1 teaspoon garlic powder
- 1 teaspoon paprika powder
- 1/4 teaspoon salt
- 1/4 teaspoon ground black pepper
- 2 teaspoons olive oil

Directions

1. Preheat oven to 400°F (200°C).
2. In a bowl, mix eggs and buttermilk.
3. In a second bowl, add flour, breadcrumbs, garlic powder, paprika powder, salt and black pepper. Mix until well combined.
4. Dip the chicken cubes into the egg mixture. Next into the breading mixture.
5. Place the breaded chicken on a baking sheet lined with parchment paper. Drizzle the chicken with olive oil.
6. Place chicken in oven and bake, about 30 minutes or until crispy and golden brown.
7. Remove from oven and serve with your favorite dipping sauce.

Nutrition Facts
Per Serving

187 calories
Protein 21.3 g
Carbs 11.1 g
Fiber 0.6 g
Fat 6.2 g

Recipe Notes

- Serve the popcorn chicken with a low-fat Ranch dressing Greek yogurt dip.
- Substitute butter milk for soy milk if you're lactose intolerant.
- You can also use an air fryer instead of the oven. Use the same temperature and cooking time.

Roasted Edamame Beans

Yield: 4 servings

Time: 25 minutes

☑ Solid Foods

☐ Soft Foods

☐ Pureed Foods

☐ Full Liquids

Ingredients

- 1 tablespoon olive oil
- 1/2 teaspoon garlic powder
- 1/2 teaspoon onion powder
- 1/2 teaspoon salt
- 1/4 teaspoon ground black pepper
- 1 cup (150 g) ready to eat edamame beans

Directions

1. Preheat oven to 375°F (190°C).
2. In a bowl, add olive oil, garlic powder, onion powder, salt and black pepper. Stir until well combined.
3. Line a baking sheet with parchment paper.
4. Place edamame on baking sheet and drizzle olive oil mixture over the edamame beans. Toss until all edamame beans are fully coated.
5. Place baking sheet in middle of oven and bake until crispy, about 15 minutes. Stir edamame beans halfway through baking.
6. Serve warm as a side dish or cooled as a crispy snack.

Nutrition Facts
Per Serving

117 calories
Protein 8.1 g
Carbs 3.6 g
Fiber 5 g
Fat 6.7 g

Recipe Notes

- Try different herbs and spices to switch up the flavor.
- Herbs to try are: basil, parsley, cumin, paprika and turmeric.
- Did you know that edamame are a great source of protein with an astonishing 18 g of protein per cup?

Red Salsa Dip

🍴 Yield: 3 servings

🕐 Time: 10 minutes

☑ Solid Foods

☐ Soft Foods

☐ Pureed Foods

☐ Full Liquids

POST-OP

SLIDER FOOD HACK

Ingredients (salsa)
- 2 large tomatoes, diced
- 1/4 red onion, chopped
- 1 tablespoon parsley, chopped
- 1 tablespoon cilantro, chopped
- 1 tablespoon lemon juice
- Salt and pepper to taste

To serve
- 1 single serve packet of chips
- Or use the apple chips recipe on page 40
- Raw veggie sticks like celery, carrot and bell pepper sticks

Directions

1. In a serving bowl, add tomatoes, onion, parsley, cilantro, lemon juice, salt and pepper. Mix until well combined.
2. Serve with chips or raw veggie sticks.

Nutrition Facts
Per Serving

14 calories
Protein 0.5 g
Carbs 2 g
Fiber 0.9 g
Fat 0.2 g

Recipe Notes
- The salsa can also be used as a condiment on a whole wheat cracker or as a dip with pita bread
- Chips is considered a slider food. But when pairing it with a high-fiber food source (tomatoes), you're creating a balanced snack.
- Add chopped jalapeño to the salsa if you can tolerate spicy food well.

Spicy Pumpkin Seeds

Yield: 8 servings

Time: 20 minutes

☑ Solid Foods ☐ Pureed Foods

☐ Soft Foods ☐ Full Liquids

Ingredients

- 1 cup (100 g) raw pumpkin seeds
- 1 tablespoon olive oil
- 1/2 teaspoon paprika powder
- 1/2 teaspoon garlic powder
- 1/2 teaspoon cumin powder
- 1/4 teaspoon ground cayenne pepper

Directions

1. Preheat oven to 350°F (175°C) and line a baking sheet with parchment paper.
2. In a bowl, mix the pumpkin seeds, oil, paprika powder, garlic powder, cumin powder and cayenne pepper until well combined.
3. Spread the pumpkin seeds evenly on the baking sheet.
4. Place in middle of oven and roast until golden, stirring halfway through, about 15 minutes.
5. Serve when still warm.

Nutrition Facts
Per Serving

83 calories
Protein 3.8 g
Carbs 0.3 g
Fiber 7.1 g
Fat 1.1 g

Recipe Notes

- Pumpkin seeds can easily turn from golden brown to burnt. Make sure to check regularly during the roasting process.
- Pumpkin seeds are an excellent source of protein with about 10 grams of protein per ounce.

Cucumber Hummus Coins

Yield: 12 servings

Time: 10 minutes

✓ Solid Foods ☐ Pureed Foods

☐ Soft Foods ☐ Full Liquids

Ingredients

- 1 cucumber
- 3 tablespoons hummus
- Salt and pepper to taste

Toppings (optional)
- Sliced cherry tomatoes
- Sliced radish
- Fresh parsley

Directions

1. Cut the cucumber in 12 equal coins.
2. With a teaspoon, spoon out the core of the cucumber coins.
3. Add 1 teaspoon of hummus in the middle of the cucumber coin. Repeat this process 12 times, until all coins are filled.
4. Top with sliced cherry tomatoes, sliced radish and parsley leaves if desired.

Nutrition Facts

Per Cup

18 calories
Protein 0.5 g
Carbs 0.8 g
Fiber 0.4 g
Fat 1.4 g

Recipe Notes

- Substitute the hummus for the black bean dip recipe on page 20.
- If you can't tolerate raw vegetable peels, make sure to peel the cucumber before you start.

Crispy Kale Chips

Yield: 4 servings
Time: 30 minutes

☑ Solid Foods ☐ Pureed Foods
☐ Soft Foods ☐ Full Liquids

Ingredients

- 6 oz (150 g) kale, stems removed
- 1 tablespoon olive oil
- 1/4 cup (50 g) nutritional yeast
- Salt and peper to taste
- 1/2 cup (50 g) grated Parmesan cheese

Directions

1. Preheat oven to 350°F (175°C).
2. Wash and drain the kale thoroughly. Set aside in a colander and allow excess moisture to drip away, about 15 minutes.
3. Transfer the kale to a baking sheet and tap dry with a paper towel until excess moisture is removed.
4. In a bowl, add the kale and olive oil. Toss until fully coated.
5. Line a baking sheet with parchment paper. And place the kale on the baking sheet.
6. Sprinkle the kale with the nutritional yeast, salt and pepper and mix until distributed evenly. Make sure that the kale pieces don't overlap each other.
7. Place in oven and bake, about 15 minutes. Flipping halfway through.
8. Remove from oven and sprinkle with grated Parmesan.
9. Serve immediately for the best "crunch".

Nutrition Facts
Per Serving

129 calories
Protein 11.6 g
Carbs 5.1 g
Fiber 1.8 g
Fat 6.5 g

Recipe Notes

- Did you know that nutritional yeast is an excellent source of vitamins and minerals, and provides protein too?
- Nutritional yeast adds a nutty and somewhat 'cheesy' flavor to your dish.

FROZEN
BITES & DRINKS

Bari Berry Milkshake

✂ Yield: 4 servings

🕐 Time: 10 minutes

✓ Solid Foods   ☐ Pureed Foods

✓ Soft Foods   ☐ Full Liquids

Ingredients

- 2 cups (480 g) Greek yogurt
- handful ice cubes
- 2 cups (120 g) berries, frozen (eg. blueberries, raspberries, strawberries, cranberries)
- 1 teaspoon vanilla extract

Toppings (optional)
- Low-fat whipped cream
- Chopped berries
- Chopped mint

Directions

1. In a blender, mix yogurt, ice cubes, berries and vanilla extract on medium speed until combined evenly.
2. Pour the yogurt mixture into a glass.
3. Top with low-fat whipped cream, mint and chopped berries.

Nutrition Facts
Per Serving

83 calories
Protein 10.1 g
Carbs 9.3 g
Fiber 0.7 g
Fat 0.1 g

Recipe Notes

- If you can't tolerate cold drinks (yet) you can use fresh fruit instead of frozen fruit.
- Substitute the berries for 1 frozen banana and 1 tablespoon of peanut butter for a different variety.
- Use canned fruit, or peel the skin and soften the fruit before adding it to the yogurt - if you're in the soft foods stage. Always follow your surgeons guidelines in regard to adding fruit back to your diet.

Fresh Fruit Popsicles

 Yield: 8 servings

Prep time: 10 minutes
Freeze time: 6 hours

 ☑ Solid Foods ☐ Pureed Foods

☑ Soft Foods ☐ Full Liquids

POST-OP

NORMALIZING CARBS

Ingredients

- 2 kiwis
- 2 apples
- 1/2 cup (75 g) strawberries
- 1/2 cup (50 g) blueberries
- 1/2 cup (60 g) raspberries
- 8 oz (240 ml) water

Equipment
- Popsicle molds
- Popsicle sticks

Directions

1. Peel the kiwis and apples and cut into quarters.
2. Press the quarters kiwi and apple to the sides of the mold.
3. Add the blueberries and raspberries and fill in as many gaps as you can.
4. Press in as much of the remainder of fruit as you can.
5. Fill the mold with apple juice up until 3/4.
6. Place the popsicle sticks in the middle.
7. Place in freezer until ready.

Nutrition Facts
Per Serving

53 calories
Protein 0.5 g
Carbs 10.9 g
Fiber 1.5 g
Fat 0.2 g

Recipe Notes

- Substitute water for skimmed milk, buttermilk or soy milk if you want to add more protein to this recipe.
- Use canned fruit, or peel the skin and soften the fruit before adding it to the yogurt - if you're in the soft foods stage. Always follow your surgeons guidelines in regard to adding fruit back to your diet.

Vanilla Iced Proffee

⚔ Yield 1 serving

🕐 Time 10 minutes

☑ Solid Foods ☐ Pureed Foods

☐ Soft Foods ☐ Full Liquids

Ingredients

- 1 espresso shot
- 1 teaspoon cocoa powder
- 8 oz (240 ml) (high protein) milk product
- 1/2 teaspoon vanilla extract
- Handful ice cubes
- 1 tablespoon low-fat whipped cream

Directions

1. Brew espresso and let it cool off.
2. In a bowl, combine the whipped cream and vanilla extract.
3. In a blender, add coffee, 1/2 ice cubes, milk and cocoa powder. Blend until smooth.
4. Pour proffee into a glass.
5. Add other 1/2 ice cubes.
6. Top proffee with vanilla whipped cream.

Nutrition Facts
Per Serving

109 calories
Protein 9.7* g
Carbs 1.7g
Fiber 0 g
Fat 5.3 g

*Amount of protein can be higher when using a high protein product or if you add protein powder to your proffee

Recipe Notes

- Caffeinated beverages are typically advised against in the first 30 days after bariatric surgery. Be sure to check in with your surgeon before adding any caffeine to your diet.
- Substitute milk for soy milk if you're looking for a high-protein plant based variety.
- Stevia is a substitute for sugar made from the leaves of the Stevia plant.

Creamy Banana Ice Cream

 Yield 4 servings

 Prep time: 5 minutes
Freeze time: 3 hours

☑ Solid Foods   ☐ Pureed Foods

☑ Soft Foods   ☐ Full Liquids

Ingredients

- 2 bananas
- 2 tablespoons low-fat cream cheese
- 8 walnuts, crushed

Toppings (optional)
- Dark chocolate chips
- Cinnamon powder
- Chopped walnuts

Directions

1. In a blender, add the bananas and cream cheese. Blend until smooth.
2. Transfer banana mixture in freezer container and stir in walnuts.
3. Place in freezer for at least 6 hours.
4. Top with chocolate chips, cinnamon powder and chopped walnuts.

Nutrition Facts
Per Serving

147 calories
Protein 3.5 g
Carbs 9.2 g
Fiber 1.4 g
Fat 10.3 g

Recipe Notes

- Omit the walnuts and chocolate chips if you're still in the soft foods stage.
- Add cocoa powder to the mixture to satisfy a chocolate craving perfectly.
- Substitute low-fat cream cheese for soy yogurt for a vegan variety.

Frozen Yogurt Bark

🍴 Yield: 10 servings

🕐 Prep time: 15 minutes
Freeze time: 3 hours

✓ Solid Foods
☐ Soft Foods

☐ Pureed Foods
☐ Full Liquids

POST-OP

SLIDER FOOD HACK

Ingredients

- 2 cups (480 g) Greek yogurt
- 1 teaspoon vanilla extract
- 1 1/2 cup (225 g) strawberries, thinly sliced
- 1/8 cup (20 g) dark chocolate chips

Directions

1. Line a rimmed baking sheet with parchment paper
2. In a bowl, stir yogurt and vanilla extract.
3. Spread the yogurt mixture on the prepared baking sheet.
4. Add the strawberries evenly on top and sprinkle with chocolate chips.
5. Place in freezer until firm, at least 3 hours.
6. To serve, cut or break into equal pieces.

Nutrition Facts
Per Serving

45 calories
Protein 4.3 g
Carbs 4.1 g
Fiber 0.9 g
Fat 0.5 g

Recipe Notes

- Substitute the strawberries for other fruit.
- Did you know that yogurt is a natural probiotic that supports gut health after bariatric surgery?
- Chocolate is considered a slider food. When pairing it with a high-protein food source like Greek yogurt, you're creating a balanced snack without demonizing chocolate. It's a win-win!

PORTABLE
BITES

Egg & Broccoli Muffins

Yield: 6 servings

Total time 40 minutes

☑ Solid Foods   ☐ Pureed Foods

☑ Soft Foods   ☐ Full Liquids

Ingredients

- 1 broccoli, without stem, florets taken apart
- 3 eggs, whole
- 2 egg whites
- 1/4 cup (60 g) cheddar, shredded
- 1/4 cup (25 g) parmesan, grated
- 1 teaspoon olive oil
- Salt and pepper to taste

Directions

1. Preheat oven to 350°F (175°C).
2. In a pan, steam broccoli, about 6 minutes, until softened.
3. Remove broccoli from pan and break into smaller pieces.
4. Spray a non-stick cupcake tin with cooking spray and spoon broccoli evenly into 6 tins.
5. In a bowl, beat eggs, egg whites, cheese, salt and pepper.
6. Pour the mixture into the greased tins on top of the broccoli until 3/4 full.
7. Top with grated cheddar and bake in the oven, about 20 minutes.

Nutrition Facts
Per Serving

116 calories
Protein 9 g
Carbs 0.3 g
Fiber 0.7 g
Fat 8.5 g

Recipe Notes

- You can use any size cupcake tin mold. Be sure to adjust the portions accordingly.
- Use the muffins as a gram-and-go snack or small meal.

Lentil Hummus Dip

 Yield: 4 servings

Time: 10 minutes

 ☑ Solid Foods
☑ Soft Foods

 ☑ Pureed Foods
☐ Full Liquids

POST-OP

NORMALIZING CARBS

Ingredients

- 1/2 cup (85 g) canned chickpeas, drained
- 1/2 cup canned lentils (85 g), drained
- 1 garlic clove, crushed
- 1 tablespoon tahini
- 2 tablespoons olive oil
- 1/2 teaspoon cumin powder
- 1 teaspoon paprika powder
- Salt and pepper to taste
- Lemon juice to taste

Serve with:
- Celery sticks
- Bell pepper sticks
- Cucumber slices
- Carrot sticks
- Whole grain crackers

Nutrition Facts
Per Serving

121 calories
Protein 4.1 g
Carbs 7.4 g
Fiber 3.2 g
Fat 7.7 g

Directions

1. In a food processor or blender, mix all the ingredients until well combined. Add 1-3 tablespoons of water until desired texture.
2. Add salt and pepper to taste.
3. Transfer hummus in a small air-tight container to-go.
4. Add salt, pepper and a splash of lemon juice to taste.
5. Serve with raw vegetable sticks or whole grain crackers.

Recipe Notes

- Adjust herbs and spices to your needs when in the pureed/soft foods stage - blend well. Omit the raw vegetable sticks and the crackers.
- Did you know that all legumes are an excellent source of plant based protein?
- Slice your favorite raw vegetables and pack in a closed container with your pea dip for a delicious snack on the go!

Turkey Pinwheels

✂ Yield: 15 pinwheels

🕐 Time: 15 minutes

☑ Solid Foods   ☐ Pureed Foods

☐ Soft Foods   ☐ Full Liquids

Ingredients

- 3 oz (90 g) low-fat cream cheese, softened
- 3 tablespoons cheddar, grated
- 1 tablespoon parsley, chopped
- 1 tablespoon chives, chopped
- 12 cooked deli turkey slices
- 3 lettuce leaves
- 3 whole grain wraps, small
- Salt and pepper to taste

Directions

1. In a bowl, mix cream cheese, cheddar and herbs.
2. Spread a layer of cheese mixture on a wrap and add 4 turkey slices on top.
3. Add lettuce leaves.
4. Roll the wrap tightly and cut into 5 equal slices.
5. Continue this process with all 3 wraps.

Nutrition Facts
Per Serving

65 calories
Protein 4.6 g
Carbs 4.8 g
Fiber 0.3 g
Fat 3 g

Recipe Notes

- Substitute turkey slices for canned tuna.
- Try different herbs and spices to change flavours.
- Can't tolerate wraps? Substitute the wrap for Romaine lettuce leaves.
- Substitute whole grain wraps for veggie wraps.
- Top the wraps with Sriracha sauce to spice it up.

Tuna Patties

⚔ Yield: 8 servings

🕐 Time: 30 minutes

☑ Solid Foods

☐ Soft Foods

☐ Pureed Foods

☐ Full Liquids

Ingredients

- 2 5 oz (140 g) cans tuna, in brine and drained
- 2 teaspoons mustard
- 1/4 (10 g) cup breadcrumbs
- 1/2 teaspoon lemon zest
- 1/2 tablespoon lemon juice
- 1 tablespoon water
- 2 tablespoons fresh parsley
- 1/4 cup (25 g) fresh scallion, chopped
- 1 egg
- 1 tablespoon olive oil
- Salt and pepper to taste

Dipping sauce (optional)
- Low-fat Greek yogurt

Directions

1. In a bowl, mix the tuna, mustard, breadcrumbs, lemon zest, lemon juice, water, parsley, spring onion until well combined.
2. Next, mix in the egg with the tuna mixture.
3. Divide the mixture in 8 equal parts. Flatten to turn into patties.
4. Line a baking tray with parchment paper and place the patties on the tray.
5. In a skillet, heat olive oil. Bake the patties until golden brown, about 6 minutes. Flip the patties halfway through the baking process.

Nutrition Facts
Per Serving

64 calories
Protein 9.7 g
Carbs 1.1 g
Fiber 0.1 g
Fat 2.3 g

Recipe Notes

- Substitute the tuna with crab meat for a different variety.
- Let the patties chill in the fridge for about 1 hour before baking them to create more firmness.
- Use an air fryer or oven instead of a pan, 350°F (175°C), about 7 minutes.

Caprese Salad Sticks

X Yield: 8 servings

☐ Time: 15 minutes

☑ Solid Foods   ☐ Pureed Foods

☐ Soft Foods   ☐ Full Liquids

Ingredients

- 8 grape tomatoes, halves
- 8 mini mozzarella balls
- 8 basil leaves
- Salt and pepper to taste

Topping (optional)
- Balsamic vinegar

Directions

1. Thread one half of cherry tomato, 1 mozzarella ball, the other half of cherry tomato and 1 basil leaf on a (tooth)pick.
2. Repeat the process until all ingredients are used up
3. Drizzle with balsamic vinegar.

Nutrition Facts
Per Serving

28 calories
Protein 2 g
Carbs 0.5 g
Fiber 0.2 g
Fat 2 g

Recipe Notes

- If you can't find pre-packed small mozzarella balls, make your own mini-balls instead using a regular mozzarella piece.
- Did you know that basil contains *eugenol*, which can help lower blood pressure?

Protein Coconut Balls

Yield: 10 servings
Time: 10 minutes

☑ Solid Foods
☐ Soft Foods
☐ Pureed Foods
☐ Full Liquids

Ingredients

- 1 cup (75 g) unsweetened coconut flakes
- 1/2 cup (80 g) rolled oats
- 2 scoops (vanilla) protein powder
- 1 tablespoon coconut oil
- 1/4 teaspoon coconut extract

Directions

1. In a food processor, add 4/5 cup of coconut flakes, rolled oats, protein powder, coconut oil and coconut extract. Pulse until combined.
2. Remove coconut batter using a cookie scoop and place scoops on surface.
3. Roll coconut batter into balls.
4. Roll each coconut ball in remainder of coconut flakes.

Nutrition Facts
Per Serving*

75 calories
Protein 1.4 g
Carbs 5.1 g
Fiber 1.4 g
Fat 12.9 g

*Nutritional value is calculated without the protein powder

Recipe Notes

- Try different flavors protein powder for different varieties.
- Substitute coconut oil for peanut butter.

Rice Paper Shrimp Rolls

Yield: 4 servings

Time: 10 minutes

☑ Solid Foods

☐ Soft Foods

☐ Pureed Foods

☐ Full Liquids

POST-OP

NORMALIZING CARBS

Ingredients

- 4 8-inch (22 cm) rice paper wrappers
- 4 oz (115 g) pre-cooked shrimp
- 4 lettuce pieces

Dipping sauce (optional)
- Hoi sin sauce
- Peanut sauce

Directions

1. In a bowl, add water and 1 piece of rice paper. Allow to soak for 10 seconds.
2. Remove rice paper from bowl and place on surface.
3. Add 1 piece of lettuce, then 1/4 of the shrimp.
4. Repeat steps 1-3 for the other 3 pieces of rice paper.
5. Gently, but firmly, roll the loaded shrimp rolls.
6. Serve with your favorite dipping sauce.

Nutrition Facts
Per Serving

57 calories
Protein 5.7 g
Carbs 6.1 g
Fiber 0.5 g
Fat 0.5 g

Recipe Notes

- Substitute the rice paper wrappers for sea weed wrappers if you can't tolerate rice paper well.
- Add more raw vegetables to your shrimp roll, like carrots, cucumber, scallion and bell pepper.
- Substitute the shrimp for tofu if you're looking for a vegan variety.
- Pack your shrimp rolls to-go.

Made in the USA
Monee, IL
01 October 2022

14984716R00059